CW01150352

JUST NEVER GIVE UP

AN UNLIKELY PERSON FOLLOWING GOD INTO UNLIKELY PLACES

DAVID L. SEBASTIAN

Advance Praise for *Just Never Give Up...*

This memoir should be read by those who are contemplating vocational ministry and especially those who are discouraged in their ministry journey. Those who are not in vocational ministry would also benefit from this book as it will provide them with compassionate understanding of the struggles that pastors experience. This book brings wonderful insight into the life of one who has committed his life to the proclamation of Jesus as the Christ, the Son of God.

> MaryAnn Hawkins, Dean
> Anderson University
> School of Theology

We've often heard that "the call to serve is the call to prepare." David Sebastian heard both calls....

In this wonderful memoir of a Christ follower, you will find many clues to the faithful life of ministry. I am delighted to commend it to you!

> James L. Edwards, President Emeritus
> Anderson University

David Sebastian humbly helps us to see God's hand on a life surrendered. He then shows us how that same transforming power is available to all of us.

David Sebastian's life experiences reflect the depth of commitment to his Lord, his wife, his family and the church.

> Jeff Jenness, President
> Servant Solutions, Inc.

Refreshing transparency is the hallmark of David Sebastian's life story. *Just Never Give Up* is truly a testament to what it means to persevere as one follows the leadership of the Holy Spirit. Those of us who were privileged to experience David's leadership would never know parts of his journey without this memoir. Thank you, David, for never giving up!

> Diana L. Swoope, Senior Pastor
> Arlington Church of God
> Akron, Ohio

It is a rare privilege to meet your heroes. Rarer still to know them as friends. *Just Never Give Up* will allow you to do both with David and Debbie Sebastian.... Their story only makes you love them more.

> Paul Strozier, Senior Pastor
> Madison Park Church of God
> Anderson, Indiana

David's story is inspiring, one filled with change from the moment of his calling at age twenty, through several decades of change in the culture and in the church. With a clear calling, unwavering commitment to the gospel of Jesus Christ, and a true partner in life, David Sebastian just never gave up!

> G. David Cox and Jan Cox, Retired
> Indianapolis, Indiana

Everybody has a story and every story is hinged on the choices we make. *Just Never Give Up* is a story of achievement, blessing, and promise, still unfolding, made possible by a sure-footed commitment to follow through every time, never running away....It is a story that calls the better out of all of us.

> Jim Lyon, General Director
> Church of God Ministries, Inc.

JUST NEVER GIVE UP

AN UNLIKELY PERSON FOLLOWING GOD INTO UNLIKELY PLACES

DAVID L. SEBASTIAN

JORDAN*publishing*
innovative christian resources

Just Never Give Up: An Unlikely Person Following God into Unlikely Places. Copyright © by David L. Sebastian. All rights reserved. Without limiting the rights of copyright here reserved, no part of this publication may be reproduced, stored in or introduced into a retrieval system, or transmitted, in any form or by any means (electronic, mechanical, photocopying, recording, or otherwise) without the prior written permission of the publisher. Please direct such requests to:

> Rights and Permissions
> Jordan Publishing
> P.O. Box 3043
> Anderson, Indiana 46018-3043

ISBN 978-1-891314-13-1 (paperback)
ISBN 978-1-891314-14-8 (hardcover)

Printed in the United States of America.

Jordan Publishing titles are available through Amazon.com, BarnesandNoble.com, and other leading book retailers.

Contents

Introduction ix

1. Following God 11
2. Discerning God's Call 17
3. Familiar Failures and Fears 20
4. Arguing with God 26
5. For Better or Worse 30
6. Academic Journey 34
7. The Discipline of Work 37
8. The Gift of Children 40
9. Angels Unaware 46
10. Learning to Lead 53
11. The Burdensome Joy 58
12. Signs and Wonders 61
13. A Season for Everything 66
14. A Bumpy Landing 70
15. Déjà Vu 76
16. Ready or Not 84

17. The Bonus Years..88
18. A Credo of Hope 95
Epilogue 105

Introduction

As I move into the winter season of my life, I want to pass on to others—particularly my children and grandchildren—the story of my professional life. While a life story is always more than one chapter, the first chapter of this book sets the theme for all the rest: an unlikely person following God into unlikely places.

Like others who undertake to write their life stories, I have been challenged to move out of my comfort zone and confront the times when I considered giving up. Along the way, I have learned that regardless of our age or stage in life, we must never give up following God.

> David L. Sebastian
> Anderson, Indiana

1. Following God

My family is the joy of my life. These are the people who know me the best and still love me the most. Members of my immediate family have not always seen eye-to-eye on many things. However, I think it is safe to say we collectively agree that our favorite family movie is, *What About Bob?* Bob is a zany character, so nervous that he fears his bladder may burst at any moment. Bob weasels his way into the family of his psychiatrist and drives Dr. Leo Marvin insane with his many neurotic demands.

My favorite line of the movie is spoken when Bob literally saves the life of the renowned psychiatrist Dr. Marvin. When Dr. Marvin chokes, Bob performs a clumsy version of the Heimlich maneuver that dislodges a piece of food from the doctor's throat. This act of heroism further embeds Bob in the family's favor (though not in Dr. Marvin's). When interviewed regarding this, Bob exclaims, "I just never gave up!"

"I just never gave up" continually makes its way into our family's conversation. Anytime we face one of life's formidable moments, we think of Bob Wiley saying this and we resolve to do the same.

The call to persevere is a universal theme in our family memory. While I have faced my share of bumps, bruises, and befuddling moments that could have discouraged me, when I chose not to give up I found a high degree of satisfaction on the other side of those difficult moments.

One Ordinary Day

It was a cold January 9, 1972. I had finished a long day working with frustrated customers because the frigid temperatures had not only stalled their cars but their lives as well. I was the owner operator of a service station in Middletown, Ohio. Two years earlier, I received an "early out" of the Army to go to college and enrolled at Miami University, declaring a business major. In the spring of 1970, when I had the opportunity to buy my brother-in-law's service station, I dropped out of college. To add another milestone to that eventful year, I was married on August 8, 1970.

My plan was to follow in the footsteps of my father, H.C. Sebastian; my three uncles, Walter Patrick, Walter Sebastian, and Charles Sebastian; four older brothers, Paul, Herb, Pat, and Jerry Sebastian; and my sister's husband Larry Mitchell to become an automotive entrepreneur. This had been my plan since eighth grade when I wrote my career book about owning a service station. After all, this was what a Sebastian was destined to do!

After work on that frigid January day, I washed up, put on a fresh set of clothes, and went to church. My pastor had invited Dr. Boyce Blackwelder, a New Testament scholar from Anderson School of Theology, to speak at a series of nightly meetings. I didn't know what a New Testament scholar was and I certainly had no idea what a "School of Theology" could be. But Debbie and I sang in the choir, were volunteer youth counselors and took our responsibilities at church quite seriously, so I determined to attend as many of the special services as possible.

Debbie was in her first year of teaching at Franklin High School in Franklin, Ohio.

At one time all of my brothers worked in my father's auto service business. The summer this picture was taken I also began working at the age of 12. One by one, each brother and my brother-in-law all started businesses of their own. Sitting is my father Herbert Clarence Sebastian. Standing from left to right Pat Sebastian, Jerry Sebastian, Paul Sebastian, Larry Mitchell and Herb Sebastian.

Because of her heavy teaching load, she was not able to attend church services on this particular night, so I called and told her I would be home right after service, when we could catch up on our busy day. Little did we know that we would end up having the first of many life-shaping conversations that evening.

Divine Encounters

I do not remember much about that evening service. It was customary to have a time for personal reflection after the message, and I remember being impressed to go down to the kneeling rail (altar) for a time of personal prayer. I had been sensing God's call into some form of full-time Christian service, but I kept this to myself for several reasons.

First, if I said yes to God's call, I would need to go to college to prepare for such a new direction in my life. I resisted this idea because I had now become a husband and I believed a man's first duty was to be the provider in his home. I had seen this modeled by my father and other significant men in my life. If I went to school as a married adult, I would put the burden of provider on Debbie, and my pride resisted the thought.

Second, I had been a poor high school student. I barely had adequate grades to graduate from high school. In a panic, I then enrolled at Miami University-Middletown. The Vietnam conflict was in full swing and without a student deferment I could end up in the rice fields of Vietnam. Needless to say, without appropriate preparation I flunked out of college and was drafted into the Army. Therefore, the idea of going back to college seemed unreasonable and financially irresponsible.

During the response time at the end of the worship service, I prayed fervently about this dilemma. I said, "God, if this is what you want me to do, then confirm it to me. Otherwise, I might do something that will embarrass both you and me." I got up from my knees and went back to my seat in the choir. When I sat down, fellow choir member Clyde Cruse whispered to me, "David, when I was about your age, I felt God calling me to full-time Christian service. While I have felt very fulfilled as an engineer, I always wondered whether I missed out on something very important." I was stunned. I hadn't said a word to Clyde about my sense of calling. Might God be using Clyde to clarify my call? I knew

God worked in mysterious ways, but this seemed mysteriously quick to me!

2. Discerning God's Call

When I arrived home, I said nothing to Debbie about my divine encounter. We talked about our day and then prepared to go to bed. We both had an early morning and a full day ahead. Just before dropping off to sleep, Debbie asked out of the blue, "Do you believe you are doing with your life what God wants you to do?"

I was totally startled, but I said, "No, I don't think so."

She asked, "What do you believe God would have you to do?"

I paused for a moment, trying to choose my words carefully. Then I replied sheepishly, "I don't know. What do you think I should do?"

"Do you think that God might be calling you into full-time Christian ministry?" she asked.

I said, "I have been wondering about that for the past year, but what will others think about me and my responsibility as a husband? And I have debilitating doubts about going to college. What if I fail again?"

Debbie encouraged me to talk with our pastor. She thought he might help me discover what a call from God is like. Needless to say, I spent the rest of the night in sleepless questioning. What could this all

In the spring of 1970 I opened up my own Sohio Dealerships. The first one was in Springboro, Ohio and the second was in Middletown, Ohio.

mean? I was terrified, but at the same time thrilled to think that a new adventure might lie ahead.

The next morning, I scheduled an appointment with my pastor, J. Herschel Caudill. When I told him what I was sensing in my life, he talked with me about the importance of having both an internal and external call. An *internal call* has to do with an individual's own feelings and inclinations about doing what God would have that person do. An *external call* is evident when other people begin to say things to the individual about that person's gifts, abilities, and opportunities for the future. Pastor Caudill reminded me that an internal and external call are both necessary so we are not self-deceived.

"David, I have been anticipating this conversation with you," my pastor said. "I have believed for some time that God was calling you into the ministry."

When he spoke those words, I recalled a moment in my early teens when I was pumping gas into his car. Pastor Caudill came to the back of the car, looked me in the eye, and tugged at my jacket, say-

18 ▪ JUST NEVER GIVE UP

ing, "David, when you grow up, I think you might become a preacher!"

At the time, I had dismissed his sentiments and never had any inclination to become a preacher. Now the memory vividly came to mind.

Before I left his house that morning, Pastor Caudill said, "David, you need to go to college. If you want, I'll help you discover where you should enroll."

My new excitement resurrected an old fear.

3. Familiar Failures and Fears

Over the next week, I began to tell my family, church friends, and employees I would be selling my business and going into the ministry. I told them that, in all probability, this would require moving from Ohio to enroll in college. Since I was thinking about ministry in the Church of God, Pastor Caudill suggested I attend a Church of God college in order to be formed in my church's tradition.

With his help, I began focusing on Anderson College in Indiana, Warner Pacific College in Oregon, Gulf Coast Bible College in Texas, and Warner Southern College in Florida. I eventually narrowed my choices to Anderson College and Warner Southern College.

Then began the application process. Each school required a high school transcript and letters of recommendation. I recall going to my high school to request a transcript to be forwarded to my selected colleges. I asked for a personal copy and nearly fainted when I saw my high school grade point average. Every college application I had examined required at least a 2.5 grade point average; sadly, my GPA was below that minimum. My dread reemerged in full force and choked my enthusiasm. Maybe this wasn't to be after all. Now I wished I had not told everybody I was going to college or entering the ministry!

In high school, I had not taken college preparatory classes because I did not plan to go to college. I'd never had a conversation with my parents or any family member about going to college. My family had a tremendous work ethic and entrepreneurial spirit, but college was not our customary life path. When I foolishly went to the community college right out of high school, I had no conversation with my parents about it. I suppose they were glad because it would keep me from being drafted, but we didn't weigh the pros and cons of the decision beforehand.

I continued to work a 48-hour week in my father's business to underwrite my tuition. Needless to say, such a schedule did not leave much time for study. When I flunked out of community college, my dad gave his first and only academic advice: "Son, you do not have to go to college to make a good living." He then talked with me about developing a plan that would allow me to go into business for myself after I returned from the Army.

My dad was correct, college is not for everyone. Many people live wonderful lives without going to college. I know many personally. But what my dad didn't know—and was therefore unable to pass on to me—is that on average, over a lifetime, a college graduate will earn nearly twice as much income as a high school graduate. Even in ordained ministry, clergy with a baccalaureate degree or master's degree will earn more than those who have only a high school diploma or a few college credits. While income is not the motivating factor for ministry, to be able to provide for your family is an important consideration.

Family Factors

My dad, Herbert Clarence Sebastian, was born in Appalachia—specifically, in Morgan County, Kentucky—on October 9, 1905. He was the first of seven children born to Asa Edward Sebastian and Sara Jane Wells. My grandfather and grandmother were farmers and worked a small plot of land. My father graduated from the eighth grade at the age of eighteen in Cannel City, Kentucky.

As a teenager, my dad plowed fields with a mule for fifty cents a day. He determined the back-breaking work of a farmer was not for him so ironically he decided go to work in the dark and dangerous coal mines in Cannel City, Kentucky. He soon discovered his experience with driving mules on the farm came in handy. This ability to drive a mule got him what he felt was a less dangerous job transporting coal instead of mining coal with the Cannel Coal Company. Later when the mine production began to slow down, he got a job with the Ohio-Kentucky Railroad. He enjoyed his work on the railroad where he was given the nickname of "Spider" because of the way he could maneuver himself on top of the railroad cars even when the cars were moving at a high rate of speed.

While working on the railroad, he began to court Nellie Marie Patrick, one of the daughters of Charley and Angelina Patrick.

My four older brothers and one older sister. Sitting from left to right are Pat, Karen and I. Standing from left to right are Herb, Jerry and Paul. I have one additional brother (Dale) who died in infancy. When I was born Paul, Herb and Pat were already married. Jerry was married and left home when I was four. Karen and I grew up together.

Herbert Clarence Sebastian and Nellie Marie Patrick (center) were married on November 23, 1923 in Cannel City, Kentucky. To the right of my mother are two of her younger sisters Stella and Ruby Patrick. To the left of my father is one of my mother's older brothers Walter Patrick.

Charley was a trader of horses and just about anything else he could buy and sell for a profit. Charley and Angelina also ran a boarding house where traveling salesmen would stay when passing through Wolf County.

Nellie was in her early teens. She famously said, "I used to put my toy dolls away when your dad would come over to see me." When my father was eighteen, he asked Grandpa Patrick if he could marry Nellie. My grandpa is reported to have said, "Well, she can't cook or do much around the house, but if you want her you can have her." My mother dropped out of school in grade six at the age of fourteen and they were married on November 23, 1923. I am sure many people wondered if the marriage would last. While life was not easy, they were married for sixty-three years before a major stroke took her life. Their marriage spoke of commitment even in challenging times. As a couple, they just never gave up!

4. Arguing with God

In late winter of 1972, I sent my college application to Anderson College and Warner Southern College. I continued working long hours in my service station, consciously saving all the money I could to invest in our new adventure. My parents had taught me to be financially responsible. Since I was twelve years old, I bought my own clothes, paid for my own dry cleaning, and purchased my own car and car insurance. The thought never crossed my mind to ask my parents for support for college or to seek a student loan. I had learned that if I wanted something, I should work hard and save for it, so I never took out an educational loan in all my years of schooling. While a debt-free education is not a possibility for everyone, I was determined to not allow debt to keep me from doing what I felt I should do with my life.

Debbie and I were deeply involved in our local congregation. We attended a young marrieds' Sunday school class and were involved in the outreach efforts of the church. During the early 1970s, five couples from the young marrieds' Sunday school class went into full-time ordained ministry in the Church of God. Those years were spiritually enriching and hold such fond memories.

One afternoon I arrived home from work and checked the mailbox, where I found a letter from the Office of Admissions of Anderson College. At first, I wanted to wait for Debbie to come home so we could open the letter together. But I couldn't wait, so I cautiously opened the letter and began to read slowly the words printed on the page. After a customary greeting, the second paragraph began with the words, "I regret to inform you that your high school transcript does not give evidence of the ability to do college level work. Therefore we cannot admit you to Anderson College. Thank you for your application." I was overcome with sorrow and embarrassment.

When Debbie arrived home, I shared the discouraging letter. She said, "Well, there is still the possibility of Warner Southern. Maybe that will be our open door. Besides, winters would be nice in Florida." Her words brought some comfort because we did have a number of family and friends living in Florida.

Several days later, the correspondence from Warner Southern arrived. The letter also stated that my high school grades

Home on leave in the summer of 1968 after advanced training in the Army Signal Corps. While at home my orders were changed from Vietnam to Germany where I took part in Operation Reforger with the 24th Infantry Division. After the Soviet led invasion of Czechoslovakia, the 24th Infantry was ordered to the Czech border to deter the Soviet aggression.

were not sufficient for me to be accepted as a full-time student. My fears were confirmed. The door had closed for college and the hope of Christian ministry.

When Debbie reread the letter later that evening, she pointed out a sentence that I had overlooked. The Admissions Office at Warner Southern encouraged me to go back to my local community college, take additional courses to raise my grade-point average, then reapply as a transfer student. I could then be accepted on academic probation. I didn't want to go back to Miami University because I wanted to take Bible and theology courses. I also didn't want to make a thousand-mile move and be on probation! I was depressed and even a little angry: angry at the colleges for not accepting me, angry at myself for telling everyone I was going into ministry, and angry at God for sending mixed messages about "surrendering to the call" and then not "parting the waters" to make it possible.

I spent the next several days pouting like Elijah when the prophet received a discouraging letter from Queen Jezebel. One day, as I sat sulking at my kitchen table, it was as if God spoke to me in a still, small voice. God seemed to say, "David, haven't I called you to full-time Christian service? Don't blame me for your lack of academic maturity in high school. Don't blame these colleges for having academic standards. As a matter of fact, stop playing the blame game. Swallow your pride and prepare for the work I have called you to do!"

I shared with Debbie what I thought God was saying to me. Not once in this process had she criticized me for my past academic performance. Now she encouraged me to reenroll in the community college and promised to help me learn how to develop good study habits. Marriage's promise to stay true to one another "for better or worse" was proving more valuable than I ever thought.

5. For Better or Worse

Deborah Lynn Miller had been born on July 4, 1949 in Middletown, Ohio to James and Mary Dean Miller. After nine years, Debbie welcomed a new baby sister named Joni. The Miller girls were the pride and joy of their parents.

Debbie soon took on the characteristics of a firstborn child; she was an achiever who loved to be around people and excelled in athletics and academics. In junior high and high school, Debbie learned to play tennis and golf. She was also a cheerleader and was active in her congregation's Baptist Youth Fellowship. On top of all of this, she was always on the honor roll and in high school was a member of the National Honor Society. Through the influence of her parents and teachers, college was always part of her long-range plan. She had hopes of becoming a teacher.

The first time I saw Debbie, I was in the eighth grade; she was in the seventh. She walked into the library of Manchester Junior High School for a student council meeting. I remember thinking, "Wow, there is one cute girl!" I already had a girlfriend, but my heart always skipped a beat when I saw Debbie Miller. In junior high, we did not become boyfriend and girlfriend, but since she was a cheerleader and I was a basketball player, we were in the gymnasium together on a regular basis.

During my senior year in high school, neither Debbie nor I were "going steady" with other people, and I was told by one of Debbie's friends that she would be open to going on a date with me if I would ask. Without that inside information, I don't think I would have had the courage to ask, because she always seemed out of my league. On February 19, 1966, we had our very first date. At the end of the evening, I asked if we could go out again. She said yes and I was elated! I never dated another girl after that fantastic February night. That spring brought a watershed moment in my relationship with Debbie Miller. There was a high school dance where the girls invited the boys to go, and I thought there might be a chance that Debbie would ask me. We had only been dating for a couple of months and I had not gotten around to telling Debbie that out of religious conviction I did not go to dances. In fairness, I felt I needed to let her know this so she could make other plans if she wanted to go. Although I dreaded the possible outcome, this would not be the first time a high-

Our wedding took place at First Baptist Church of Middletown, Ohio on August 8, 1970. The wedding party from left to right (floor level) consists of friends of the bride, Donna, Jatana, and Carol, and family of the groom Ronnie (cousin), Danny (cousin), Tom (nephew). Standing from left to right (second level) friend of the bride Judy, maid of honor and sister Joni, bride Debbie, groom David, best man and brother Jerry and brother-in-law Larry.

school dating relationship was terminated because of my religious convictions.

To my utter astonishment, when I explained this, she said, "The spring dance is not a deal breaker." I can't explain what that conversation meant to me. I had begun to fear that my religious convictions would somehow be a line of demarcation in any long-term relationship. Not only did I sit out the dances, but I did not drink alcohol, do drugs, smoke tobacco, gamble or party. These behaviors were part and parcel of the social climate of our high-school culture in the 1960s. While not agreeing with all of these religious convictions, Debbie nonetheless accepted me and my convictions. I never thought I would experience that kind of acceptance. I was blown away.

Debbie was the first person I met who could accept someone without necessarily approving of their beliefs and behaviors. This required her to move outside of her upbringing to appreciate the cultural backgrounds of other people. Understanding the difference between acceptance and approval has been an ongoing conversation in our marriage. The conversation continues because we do believe there is such a thing as absolute truth. We don't believe in moral relativism, in which everyone is entitled to their own "truth" without question. However, when sincere people are honestly seeking truth, Debbie and I believe we must give them time and space to discern the truth, and trust that God will reveal the truth to them. In many ways, we have been guided by the motto, "In essentials, unity; in non-essentials, liberty; in all things, charity."

6. Academic Journey

Debbie confidently told me I had the ability to do college work but, in her opinion, I had never really applied myself and had not developed good study habits. She said she could help me do that; after all, she was an honor student and now a professional educator. She could not motivate me because motivation was something internal, but Debbie insisted that motivation coupled with discipline could overcome many obstacles. After wallowing in self-pity for a couple of weeks after I got the rejection letters from Anderson and Warner Southern, I decided to try again. I resolved to become a good student.

I went back to Miami University and enrolled in classes. With Debbie's help, I studied hard. I read and reread book chapters. I prepared diligently for examinations. Painstakingly, I learned to write academic papers. I recall receiving my first mid-term grades and finding to my astonishment that I had over a 3.0 GPA. I was on my way.

In the fall quarter of 1972, I was able to transfer one year of college credit to Warner Southern College, where I was accepted as a sophomore on academic probation. With the help of dedicated faculty members and the ongoing assistance of Debbie, my personal tutor and typist, I was able to excel. I discovered a love for learning. I came across a term in one of my education courses that shed light on what was happening: *the law of readiness.* In my years as a pastor and later as an academic dean, this has been a helpful concept to share. It offers a word of encouragement to people struggling with any academic pursuit. When I have shared my embarrassing struggle with academics and explained the law of readiness, the struggle has given other people hope, provided they would not give up.

So what is the law of readiness?

Some students who go to college right out of high school often waste time and money because they are not ready to buckle down and do the hard work required. Some high-school graduates are simply not ready for college, so I believe parents are ill-advised to treat each student the same. Some new high-school graduates would be better advised to join the military, get a job, or enlist in some form of voluntary work at home or abroad. They will discover over time what they want to do with their lives. Some parents feel this involves a risk that is too great. Maybe their daughter or son will never return to the classroom. I remind them that plunging into university life without a purpose and plan is one of the most risky things an eighteen- to twenty-two-year-old can do. Maturity, motivation, and purpose, coupled with positive friendships, can make all the difference between success or failure in life.

I lacked the maturity, even in high school, to see how a good education could help me become a good mechanic. In hindsight, being an honor student could have greatly enhanced my analytical and communications skills. For whatever reason, I was not ready for college. But going back to college at the age of twenty-five, after two years of military service and three years of self-employment, I was ready and eager to hit the books.

7. The Discipline of Work

After restarting my academic life in college and grad school, I discovered an internal conflict that followed me into my new profession as a congregational pastor. I had finally learned how to study and how to create a plan that enabled me to meet semester deadlines. (In college, you soon learn there are no parents and teachers hovering over you to make sure you do your work and ask if your research paper is ready to submit on time.) In addition, I had to develop a place and time to do my studies, and I had to guard that space and time as something sacred.

When trying to discern whether you have a call into Christian ministry, if you discover you have an aversion to study, this could be a good indicator that ministry—particularly preaching, teaching, and leading—may not be a clear path for you. These duties require you to close the door and reflect upon a given text, topic, or ministry context. Thinking and writing help to bring clarity so that you can speak and lead effectively.

I learned to value my study time because, as a minister who spoke publicly several times a week, I never wanted to fall into the trap of simply having to say something. I wanted always to have something to say. Public speaking requires a constant loading and reloading of your mind with relevant information to be shared with those who come to church and give of their valuable time to listen and to grow spiritually.

However, in my preparation time I encountered an internal conflict. When I closed my study door, the Enemy constantly whispered, "Why are you wasting time here? Don't you know that real ministry is out there with people?"

For most of my life, I had associated work with things that I did with my hands. To sit, except for moments of rest to regain physical strength, I considered wasting time. Real work produced perspiration, calloused hands, and sore muscles. Only after hard physical work could a person ever justify sitting, reading, and reflecting.

Gradually, I came to understand that true work can consist of either brain or brawn. Certain kinds of work require muscle power while others require mental exertion. Mental and physical activities are both work and can leave us exhausted, though with a degree of satisfaction, when a job is complete. All work is to be done as though we were doing it unto the Lord. When we work, we should always ask, "Is the work well done and is the Lord well pleased?"

8. The Gift of Children

For the first fifteen years of our marriage, Debbie or I or both of us had been in college or grad school. We had professional callings that required advanced preparation and this preparation required time, effort, and money. Early in our marriage, we thought we would start a family after two years; but as we contemplated our callings, we came to the conclusion that maybe we should forgo a family in order to give ourselves to our vocations. While we never discussed a "childless marriage" with our parents and friends, after eight years of not having children, many stopped asking the question, "When are you starting your family?"

Then something began to change. Perhaps Debbie began to hear the biological clock ticking loudly. I began to question my motives: Did I really want to give myself to my calling for the greater good, or did I simply want the freedom to march to my own drum beat? Whatever the influencing factors, we decided in the eighth year of our marriage that we really did want to begin a family of our own.

Having biological children is not for everyone and for some families it is a physical impossibility, but for us it was one of the best and most satisfying gifts we could ever imagine. After living for eight years as a couple and doing things in our own time and way, we discovered that having children required sacrifice and patience. For us, eight years of married life without children helped us to mature and get ready for the next adventure.

On May 25, 1978, Debbie and I were sitting on the back porch in the late afternoon, cracking walnuts. Debbie's labor pains started and we knew it was time to head for the hospital. She was in labor for twelve hours when suddenly the baby's heart monitor began to alarm. Doctors and nurses rushed into the room and informed me that our baby's heart rate had dropped so radically that they needed to take both mother and baby for an emergency C-section. After about forty-five minutes of agonizing loneliness in the waiting room, I was approached by a nurse who said, "Your wife and baby girl are doing just fine. Debbie will be in recovery for another hour, but I can take you to see your little girl." Then the nurse added with a smile, "She is beautiful."

I know a lot of people speak about their newborn as the most adorable baby in the

Our lives were blessed beyond words with our two daughters. (Julie above and Amy below). Growing up they both enjoyed sports, vacations at the beach, church activities and boys. The later enjoyment kept their father on his knees.

world, but when I saw my daughter I thought the whole world would agree with the nurse and me that Julie Kristen Sebastian was the most beautiful baby ever! Debbie and I took her home from the hospital and our lives changed. Now everything we did for the rest of our lives would be with the thought of how this might impact our daughter.

From the earliest years, Julie was a fighter. She would strive to succeed, whether it was in academics, gymnastics, or fighting for what she perceived as the rights of other people. I always felt that the umbilical cord that wrapped tightly around her neck in the womb forced her from the very beginning to fight for the right to exist. Julie had her share of challenges, but because of her tenacity, she was always able to land on her feet and make the most out of any life situation.

On December 10, 1980, we welcomed Amy Nicole Sebastian into this world. Amy's birth was less stressful than that of her older sister. Late in the pregnancy, Debbie's gynecologist recommended a C-section, so we put the birth date on our calendar. We dropped Julie off at our neighbor's house and arrived at the hospital to prepare for the delivery of our second child. Right on schedule and without any glitches, I was in the surgical suite alongside Debbie to welcome Amy Nicole.

I remember thinking throughout Debbie's pregnancy, "How will I be able to love my second child as much as the first?" That question was answered the moment I held Amy in my arms. God gives us more than enough love for all of our children. When I held my baby girl, I thought, "We are the most blessed couple in the world."

While coming from the same parents and living in the same home, Amy was a different child than her older sister. From her earliest years, she was very relaxed and loved to cuddle. However, she was very competitive on the playground. Amy loved to run races with her friends and her foot speed became a great asset in high school and college soccer. While Amy did well in school, spending hours studying never appealed to her. But what she lacked in study skills she excelled in social skills. Her "people smarts" were off the charts. Amy always had great empathy for people and would spend many volunteer hours working with young people. She always seemed to make life better for those she met.

Debbie and I have always prayed for our daughters. Specifically, we prayed for the person they would marry if they chose to marry. We prayed they would marry a man devoted to God and to our daughter. We are grateful that both Julie and Amy found someone with whom they could share life in the good times and bad. Colin and Jon, our sons-in-law, love their wives and children with a sacrificial love that brings great satisfaction to our hearts. They both are passionate about their vocations. Colin was passionate about sports and became athletic director at Anderson High School, which seemed to be a perfect fit. In high school, Jon rediscovered his love for music and became a singer-songwriter. Now he is able to share his music with people around the world.

While Debbie and I were sincere in our plans to devote our lives to our professional callings, we wholeheartedly embraced the change that included children. Although change can seem bewildering at the time, it is what brings new life. I have discovered that all of life is a series of closing certain doors and opening others. It was a blessing to be gifted with two daughters in whom we could invest ourselves for a period of time. We prayed that we would not blunder too badly in those God-given years of nurture because we longed to see our girls grow into godly women who would move into lives of their own. Even though I had preached many sermons about letting our children go, I found it a personal challenge to do so. However, beyond letting them go, we are grateful to have a few years to see their futures unfold. Whatever they do and wherever they go, they will be our beloved daughters and they will always be in our prayers for this life and the life that is to come.

9. Angels Unaware

In the fall of 1997, I was painting the interior of our house when the phone rang and Debbie informed me that the caller wanted to speak with me. As soon as he spoke, I recognized both his voice and name. In my boyhood home, Sunday mornings began by listening to the Christian Brotherhood Hour radio program, whose speaker, Dr. Eugene Sterner, had such a compelling and compassionate voice. By 1977 he had retired from the radio program to become the state minister in Colorado. Dr. Sterner asked if he could meet with Debbie and me to discuss the possibility of our pastoring the First Church of God in Phoenix, Arizona. We subsequently met with Dr. Sterner and said we would be open to begin a prayerful conversation with the church's leaders.

While in seminary, I'd had the privilege of serving the Glendale Church of God in Indianapolis, Indiana. Upon graduation, I had received a call to become full-time associate pastor with the Glendale congregation and was planning to pursue doctoral studies in Adult Education at Indiana University. I hoped to serve the church as a Minister of Christian Education or Professor of Christian Education. However, as I watched senior Pastor Dr. G. David Cox preach each week, I was captivated by his example of effective congregational preaching. My heart was stirred. However, my undergraduate and graduate studies had been in religious education, not pastoral work or preaching.

I counseled with Pastor Cox about the Phoenix opportunity. Over the past year, he had given me opportunities to preach but I felt totally inadequate. One day, Pastor Cox said to me, "If you can find satisfaction doing anything else in Christian ministry besides preaching, then do it. But if you have a deep sense that preaching is what you are called to do, then you will not be satisfied until you embrace that burden and joy. Just remember that preparation and proclamation, week in and week out, are hard work."

With this background, I began a formal conversation with the Phoenix congregation. I was only twenty-nine years of age and had little preaching experience, so I didn't think the conversation would result in my being considered as a candidate for pastor. I continued my full-time work as associate pastor at the Glendale Church of God and my part-time adjunct teaching at Anderson College, and I felt fulfilled in what I was doing.

Then two other opportunities were presented to me: In the winter of 1978, I was offered a full-time position to teach Christian Education at Anderson College. Then my home congregation invited me to join their pastoral staff to be groomed to take over for Pastor Caudill at his retirement. Four wonderful opportunities before me: What should I do?

In the spring of 1978, I boarded a plane to fly to Arizona to present myself as a candidate for the role of senior pastor. I was scheduled to preach Sunday morning and Sunday evening. In addition, over three days, I would meet with several committees and members of the congregation. Debbie was in her later months of pregnancy, so the airlines would not allow her to travel. I called her from my hotel room to explain how things were going. It was a lonely and overwhelming experience for me to grasp all by myself. The weekend concluded with the understanding the congregation would vote, according to the bylaws, in two weeks. So I got on the plane, still trying to process the weekend and my future.

The flight from Phoenix to St. Louis allowed me time to consider the decisions before me. I determined to close the conversation with my home church. I loved my home church dearly but the thought of going back home presented challenges I did not want to face in my early years. The invitation to teach at Anderson College was compelling and fit my academic preparation, but I believed I needed more years of practical experience in the church so my teaching might be more relevant to students. I declined that invitation as well.

My current position as minister of Christian Education was fulfilling with a great church and wonderful staff. Why change when things were really good? However, the burning desire to preach and lead a local congregation would not go away. On the other hand, I felt overwhelmed by feelings of fear and inadequacy.

I changed planes in St. Louis. As I boarded the plane, I took my assigned aisle seat, and a man sitting in the window seat said hello as I got settled. After takeoff, I noticed he was reviewing several Sunday worship bulletins and appeared to be making notes on each one. I thought he must be a minister. While not trying to be nosy, I recognized the names of several missionaries on the worship folders. I asked, "Do you know those people?"

He said, "Yes, the congregation I serve in San Diego supports them in our mission's budget." He extended his hand to me and said, "My name is Paul Hart. I pastor the First Church of God in San Diego, California."

I recognized his name. One of my college professors had given my name to him to serve as a possible minister of Christian Education prior to his move from Anderson, Indiana to San Diego, California. He remembered my name and asked what I was doing. I told him I had interviewed with the First Church of God in Phoenix and that the congregation and I were now praying about whether this could be a right match. Pastor Hart said he knew the Phoenix congregation very well. For the next hour and a half, we talked about the city of Phoenix and First Church of God, as well as the process of discerning God's call to a new ministry assignment. As the plane landed, I thought to myself, "Wow, was Pastor Hart God's angel of confirmation?" He had answered many of my questions about such a move. When I arrived home, I shared with Debbie every detail of the weekend, including my unexpected conversation on the plane.

After two weeks, First Church of God extended a call for us to come and serve. The majority vote was more than required by their bylaws; however, the vote was not unanimous. Evidently, some people felt my young age, lack of experience, and Midwestern cultural background made this a risky call. To be honest, I couldn't blame them. Debbie and I took a good part of the week to pray about the decision with trusted colleagues. Finally, we said yes and began to pack our bags to head west.

Discerning God's call in life can be quite perplexing. I believe the perfect will of God to be denying yourself, picking up your cross, and following Jesus. Regardless of our station in life, we Christians are called to a radical discipleship, so all of our work is divine work.

However, God does call some of us to serve in the ordained ministry of the church. God gives us freedom to discern the specific field of ministry to which he calls us. I have come to rely on conversations with trusted friends to help me discern God's call. I have also come to appreciate divine moments when God chooses to bring unexpected people such as Eugene Sterner or Paul Hart to speak into our lives. Finally, I have learned to ask, "Do I have the spiritual gift(s) for the task? Am I prepared to develop those gifts so I might succeed if I walk through this open door of Christian service?"

10. *Learning to Lead*

The ten years I spent in Phoenix, Arizona, were a lab school in leadership development. I had prepared myself professionally by going to college and seminary and by becoming an ordained minister. While these milestones were important in opening doors for ministry, they were not solely adequate to lead a congregation. I discovered to carry the title "senior pastor" was a kind of positional leadership that granted a courtesy leadership role but the true equation of leadership would require tenure plus trust.

Early on, I was fortunate to learn that my young age and lack of tenure in the congregation were inadequate to lead the congregation in any missional way. My congregational call vote percentage (88 percent) should have given me fair warning. With a little investigation, I discovered that 54 percent of the congregational members were older than me and were part of the congregation prior to my arrival. Sixteen percent were younger than me but were also already in the congregation, so they took their cues from the older group. In other words, 70 percent of the congregation was unlikely to follow my lead simply because I was the senior pastor. It took me about three years to discover that if we were going to take on any major congregational initiatives, I would have to empower key lay leaders who already had trust and tenure within the congregation.

An example of one of my most painful leadership moments occurred after I had led our Church Council through a year-long study regarding the next steps for the congregation. After careful analysis of several alternative paths forward, the Church Council made a unanimous report recommending that the congregation relocate to a growing area of the valley. A special called business meeting was held and a spirited discussion took place regarding the vote to relocate. By a 78 percent vote, the decision to relocate was made. While the affirmative vote was certainly a majority of the congregation, the heated debate and less than hoped for affirmative vote percentage left nuclear families and congregational members divided.

It is difficult to lead when there is a cloud of disappointment in the air. I felt much of the disappointment was aimed at me. Plans for relocation were made, but for a year we had no buyer for our present facility and no money available to purchase land. Then within two weeks we received a cash offer for our present property and a gift of ten acres of land for relocation. Suddenly, a beam of sunlight broke through the cloudy skies.

Debbie, the girls, and I decided to take a two-week vacation. While we were away, a petition was circulated among church members seeking a special called business meeting to rescind the vote to relocate. When I returned to my office, the signatures were on my desk. As I looked over the list, I recognized the names of several long-term members, key leaders, and major financial supporters. A special business meeting was called.

I was emotionally spent. I actually prayed that God would open a door for me

First Church of God at 9th Ave. and Fillmore in Phoenix is where I began my ministry as a senior pastor (1978-1988). In 1983, the congregation (North Hills Church) relocated to Northwest Phoenix and planted two new congregations in Glendale, Arizona and Chandler, Arizona.

to go to another place to serve. This was just too hard. I couldn't win. I loved and respected people on both sides of the issue.

When the special called business meeting was held, the sanctuary was packed. A heated discussion took place. For the first time in my tenure, some personal accusations were made about me publicly. When people voted, the choice to relocate was even stronger than before. With the wind out of my sails and no other doors opening for pastoral ministry, I prayed that God would give me wisdom and strength to lead into a somewhat fractured future.

My new task was to gather key leaders to pray and process what God would have us to do. Wonderful leaders on both sides of the issue helped turn around a decade of attendance decline by relocating the church into a growing area of the valley and planting two new congregations on both the east and west side of the valley.

Change does not come about without personal pain. However, it is important not to take things personally. People will disagree and, in some situations, be disagreeable. But with God's grace, always take the high road. Good people can disagree, but when we disagree and remain friends, the church benefits.

11. The Burdensome Joy

After a few years in Phoenix, I honestly thought I could not continue to preach week in and week out. As I began my first pastorate, I had been enthusiastic about preaching but ill-prepared for it. Since my seminary degree was in Christian Education, I had not taken a single preaching course. In my role as associate pastor, I only preached occasionally when the senior pastor was out of town. I had never faced the grind of developing and delivering two different sermons per week.

Laypeople sometimes think that standing in front of a congregation and talking is an easy thing. As an introvert, I found public speaking to be an emotionally draining experience. Then I recalled the advice of my mentor G. David Cox: "If you can do anything other than preach, then do it." No truer advice could have been given.

After seven years I was granted a sabbatical. Part of my sabbatical would be devoted to finishing my doctoral dissertation. The other part would be to relax and try to think through how I was going to deal with what Dr. James Massey calls, "The Burdensome Joy of Preaching."

I came up with a two-point strategy to deal with my burden of preaching. First of all, I decided to stop over-analyzing my preaching. During my time away from the grind of preaching, I realized that the pressure I felt was not external (that is, from congregational critics), but I was overly harsh on myself. I determined I would prepare for my preaching assignment, deliver the message to the best of my ability, and then trust the Holy Spirit to apply it to people's hearts and minds. I determined I needed to let go of my obsession with perfection and trust God to use my imperfect gift. Constant comparison erodes satisfaction. Being your best always trumps striving to be the best.

Second, I decided I needed to reach out and study formally with some of the best preachers I could find. My doctoral studies were done at Fuller Theological Seminary in Pasadena, California, where my concentration was in Evangelism and Church Growth at the School of World Mission. However, I determined to take all of my elective studies in The School of Theology in Preaching.

Taking graduate academic courses in preaching for credit forced me to read things I may not have chosen to read for myself. Academic credit allowed me to enter into a formal relationship with a professor who would critique my preparation and delivery of sermons. Such a critique was sometimes painful but always helpful. I studied homiletics and hermeneutics with John R.W. Stott, George Sweazy, Ian Pitt-Watson, and Russel Spittler. These seasoned veterans helped me to dig a deep well out of which I could draw life-giving water. Their insights and personal counsel helped me to rediscover the joy of preaching.

There still were times when I thought about quitting. It happens in every profession, including Christian ministry. Perseverance requires an inner and outward journey. The inward quest affirms our own strengths and weaknesses. We simply seek to do our best and leave the rest to God. The outward journey necessitates reaching out to others and allowing them to speak into our lives. I was so glad that when I faced the thought of giving up, I discovered people who threw out a life line. Often when we come up through the waves of discouragement and doubt we find a new future filled with opportunity and hope, provided we never give up.

12. Signs and Wonders

In June of 1987, Debbie and I attended the North American Convention of the Church of God in Anderson, Indiana. We had just completed a building fund campaign to construct a new sanctuary for the North Hills Church of God in Phoenix. Architectural drawings had been completed. However, the financial campaign didn't realize its goal, so building the new sanctuary was put on hold. While somewhat disappointed, I was pleased that church life was going well.

One evening after service at the convention, as Debbie and I returned to our dorm room, we both had a strange impression that our ten-year ministry in Phoenix may be coming to a close. Over the years I had received invitations to consider other ministry assignments, but neither Debbie nor I felt the timing was right. However, now both of us felt something was in the air. We anticipated at any moment some door was going to open and we needed to prepare ourselves to walk through it.

The entire summer of 1987, at an emotional level at least, we began preparing for a move. Debbie and I had spent a quarter of our lives in Phoenix. Our girls had spent all of their lives in Phoenix and embraced the community wholeheartedly as their home. The congregation had invested in us beyond expectation. Life was good. Even so, we had a memorable impression that God was up to something and it included us.

Summer of 1987 came and went without so much as an inkling of any door to new ministry. The Board of Elders and pastoral staff were anticipating fall and winter programs that, while not requiring my approval, should have my consent. There is nothing more agonizing than having one foot in one world and the other foot in another. To make matters worse, that "other world" had not taken shape. It only existed because of a June impression and an ongoing summer conversation with my wife.

On Labor Day morning, Debbie and I were up early having coffee on the patio. We had invited the pastoral staff over later in the afternoon for a cookout. Once again we talked about our summer impression regarding a move. We came to the conclusion that perhaps we had misinterpreted what we perceived as "God speaking" and decided to focus on the ministry at hand. But when our conversation was interrupted by the ringing of the telephone, Debbie said, "There is our answer." I picked up the phone and a voice on the other end of the line said, "David, this is God calling."

I said, "I'm listening!"

Then the serious voice on the other end turned to laughter. "David, this is Bob Reardon (former President of Anderson College). I am serving as the interim pastor of the Salem Church of God in Clayton, Ohio. I have been asked by the pulpit committee of the congregation to see if you might be open to a conversation about becoming their next senior pastor."

Given our summer impression and Debbie's comment regarding the phone call, I immediately said, "Yes, I am open to that." Dr. Reardon said that he would report back to the pulpit committee and either he or the chair of the pulpit committee would be in touch regarding next steps. I walked to the back porch and Debbie asked, "Who was that on the phone?"

I said, "God."

I explained what had happened on the phone and we both sat in utter amazement at the timing of the call.

While I have never been a "sign seeker" to prove anything about the will of God, I do believe in a God who continues to guide us.

Salem Church of God, Clayton, Ohio is where I served from 1988-1995. Salem Church helped plant new churches in Springboro, Ohio and Lake Mary, Florida during these years.

I have had several moments in life that are beyond my human explanation. For example, as a child, under the age of five years, I remember encountering an old man in a Middle Eastern robe sitting on the inside steps of my home church. Frightened, I ran to get my mother but when I returned he was gone. His image remains in my mind.

I recall as a teenager searching for days for my girlfriend's ring I had lost. While walking barefooted through my backyard, I prayed to find my ring when to my amazement it slipped onto my toe! I recollect times in my automotive business when I could not find something or diagnose some problem when help suddenly appeared. I reminisce often about my older friend who talked to me about a call to ministry when I had prayed privately just minutes before that God would give me a sign. Now the phone call and Debbie's confident affirmation, "There is our answer," simply added to a litany of God's promises to be with me.

13. A Season for Everything

I have found over the years that when God breaks into my life, those moments were not intended to prove anything about the existence of God or my favored status as a person. I have learned to accept those special moments as divine promises, not proofs.

We are tempted to think that if there is a God and if God speaks from time to time in mysterious ways, then we can be confident we are in the will of God and all of life will be easy ever after. I have discovered biblically and experientially this is not necessarily true. Even when we are in the center of God's will, we may face fiery furnaces, ferocious lions, strong head winds, and even rugged crosses.

Our time at the Salem Church of God in Clayton, Ohio, was a time to be refined by fire. The Salem Church is a great historical congregation in the Midwest. Strong and effective women and men, both ordained and non-ordained, have led the church in remarkable ways. In the 1970s, this congregation generously invested its resources to help people to become effective evangelists and competent preachers. The staff hosted creative leadership seminars that empowered church staffs across the country. The Salem Church became one of the fastest growing congregations of the Church of God in the late 1970s. The congregation purchased sixty-five acres of land and built one of the finest church facilities in North America. To be called in 1988 to serve such a congregation was an honor, and I knew I had big shoes to fill.

By the mid-1980s, Salem's miraculous growth began to subside. There were many contributing factors: The strong staff that had led such growth was no longer there. The Northwest side of Dayton, Ohio, did not develop as rapidly as anticipated. The national economy was in a downward spiral. Bank interest rates were at an all-time high. All of these mitigating factors negatively impacted attendance and offerings. The morale of the congregation was low and some wondered if the new building and large debt were worth it. Others thought it might have been better to remain in the old location where life had been good.

The next three years were personally and institutionally challenging. Our home in Phoenix, Arizona, did not sell for 3.7 years and we came close to personal bankruptcy. A dear couple, who knew nothing of our financial situation but sensing God's leading, gave us a personal financial gift which saw us through a rocky three-month period until our Phoenix house sold.

The Salem congregation was also on the brink of bankruptcy. Banks and private investors were calling for their loans and we had to cut budgets, which included reducing staff and benefits. In order to keep our bank debt, many members had to sign bank guarantee notes. Some made additional investment loans and waived the right to call their notes on demand. These sacrifices galvanized the leadership of the church to realize that indeed our trust was in God who had promised to be with us.

During those three years we began praying for a new vision to take us into the future. This vision consisted in building a new staff, instituting an annual stewardship program, planting a church in Centerville, Ohio, restructuring our debt, and planning for new debt-free athletic fields and a family life center. All of these things inspired the congregation to look to the future and enabled us to reverse the declining weekend attendance and eroding financial budget.

My time with the Salem Church of God taught me that congregations go through different seasons of life. A church leader is called to help a congregation embrace their season of the soul and to help them grow through it. The motto, "This too shall pass," reminds us that we are called to remain faithful and never give up, for God continues to lead if we have ears to hear what the Spirit is saying to the church.

14. A Bumpy Landing

On April 19, 1995, Debbie and I were in Hawaii on a long-anticipated vacation when we turned on the television to catch the news. We were shocked to see the horrifying events taking place in Oklahoma City. Someone had driven an explosives-filled truck to the front of a government building and detonated a bomb, resulting in the death of scores of innocent victims, including young children. Our hearts ached as we watched the tragedy unfold before us.

The next day, we were glued to our television watching the ongoing story from Oklahoma City when I noticed a little red light flashing on the telephone. I called the front desk and was told I had a fax from Anderson University. I had been anticipating an important communication, but was a bit surprised it was coming to me while I was in Hawaii. I went downstairs and learned it was a fax from Anderson University President James Edwards.

The fax contained an invitation to interview to become Dean of Anderson University School of Theology. Dr. Edwards had sent the fax to me in Hawaii because there were time-sensitive issues related to the end of the academic year and the next meeting of the Board of Trustees. Needless to say, our relaxing vacation in paradise came to an end even before leaving the island. As I boarded the plane, I didn't realize how quickly the tranquility of paradise would turn into personal and professional turmoil.

Actually, the seed of my angst was sown two years earlier. In November 1993 and January 1994, I had received queries from a congregation asking if I would consider interviewing for their senior pastor position. I had declined because we were in the middle of a financial campaign. In late summer, I received another call from the same church. I was told that their search committee was impressed by the Holy Spirit that I was the person for their open position. We had a confidential meeting, and Debbie and I agreed to pray about the opening; however, on the last day of 1994, I said I could not seriously discuss any potential move until spring of 1996 because of our other commitments. I realized this was a long time away and understood their need to secure pastoral leadership, but I could not promise to act sooner.

Things were going well at Salem Church of God. We had just completed a building fund campaign for a facility expansion, but did not raise enough money to begin the new project. Our congregation's leadership agreed we would not incur any additional debt and would only build when we had money in the bank. This would require us to wait another two or three years. Julie, my oldest daughter, would be entering her senior year in high school and I knew a move to another city and church would be difficult for Julie and Amy, her younger sister. So I looked forward to the new year in my role as Senior Pastor of the Salem Church of God and my volunteer assignment as Chair of Anderson University Board of Trustees.

To my surprise, the same congregation contacted me again to discuss a possible move. I said I would not even be open to discussing this until after my oldest daughter graduated from high school in May of 1996. Unfortunately, my willingness to talk again in the spring of 1996 was heard as a willingness to be their candidate in the spring of 1996. This breakdown in communication would bring about great anguish for the many people involved.

In early spring of 1995, President Edwards said my name had been submitted as a possible candidate for Dean of the Seminary. He asked if I would consider such an assignment. While I would never have submitted my name, for various reasons, I told him I would be interested because theological education had always been a passion of mine. Anderson School of Theology had a tremendous impact on my life. While in Phoenix, Arizona, I had served on the advisory board for Fuller Theological Seminary Southwest. Now, as chairman of Anderson University Trustees, I had a keen interest in the seminary and in developing leaders for the church.

Debbie and I (center) began dating in high school. Julie and Colin Short (upper right) met at Anderson University. They were married February 9, 2002. Amy and Jon McLaughlin (lower left) also met at Anderson University. They were married April 8, 2006. The Shorts have lived in Indiana and Arizona. The McLaughlin's have lived in Indiana, California and Tennessee.

A Bumpy Landing ▪ 73

On March 16, 1995, I shared with the chair of the Board of Elders at Salem Church of God that I was on a short list to be interviewed for the position of Dean. I also withdrew my name for consideration by the other church. Because of my position as Trustee Board Chair, President Edwards and I agreed that I should step down from my role on the search committee so the search process could move forward without any undue discomfort for me or the committee.

The fax I received in Hawaii on April 20, 1995 asked me to interview formally for the position of Dean. When I returned, I met with the President's Executive Staff, members of the School of Theology faculty and staff, faculty members of the undergraduate Religious Studies Department, and eventually the Board of Trustees. The meeting with the Trustees and Executive staff went well. From my perspective, the meeting with both faculties was somewhat reserved. I attributed this to the fact that many faculty members did not know me personally. Some were concerned that I had no experience of being an academic dean.

Most faculty members had heard inaccurately that a congregation had invited me to become their new pastor and that I had agreed to retract my commitment to them when I was offered the position of Dean. Other faculty members felt it was not ethical for the Chair of the Board of Trustees to become the Dean of the School of Theology. These concerns would only be resolved over a long period of time.

The immediate question was whether President Edwards, the Board of Trustees, and the General Assembly of the Church of God would give approval for David L. Sebastian to become the seventh Dean in the history of Anderson University. On May 9, 1995, I sent my letter of resignation to members of Salem Church of God, noting that the Board of Elders had released me to pursue the call to become Dean of Anderson University School of Theology.

15. Déjà Vu

An old preacher's joke goes like this: A minister of music was being considered for the staff at a very prestigious church with a thousand members. After the weekend interview, a congregational vote was taken and on Monday morning the senior pastor called the candidate. He reported, "I have some good news and bad news. The good news is of the 1,000 member's casting votes, you received 950 affirmative votes. A 95 percent vote is excellent! The bad news is the 50 negative votes came from the choir."

I was about to experience the sharp point of that joke.

The Anderson University Board of Trustees ratified my name to be forwarded to the General Assembly of the Church of God for approval as Dean of Anderson University School of Theology. In 1995, the University President and Seminary Dean were the only employees of Anderson University requiring an affirmative vote by the General Assembly before they could assume their respective positions. While my ratification was not unanimous, it was a strong vote electing me to a five-year term. My only concern was how many of the negative votes were from General Assembly members who were also members of the faculty and staff of Anderson University.

After the ratification of the General Assembly, I began to reflect on my previous ministry assignments. I never received a unanimous call to any of them. There were always some who thought I was not prepared adequately for the responsibilities I inherited. I do recall ministry peers receiving unanimous votes from their constituents, and I am sure those strong endorsements provided encouragement as they began a new work. On the other hand, I had begun each new assignment knowing I had critics. Perhaps these critics helped me to proceed with caution and to not take anything for granted.

I noticed a second pattern as well: I had always been called to assignments that required a turnaround of the ministry. One could argue that when things are at a low point, there is only one way to go—up. On the other hand, there is the real possibility that an organization can fail and you never want to be leading an organization that closes on your watch. As I reflected on my ministerial career, I began to realize that something within my personality likes these challenges. Maybe I was wired to be patient and persistent.

On July 5, 1995, I packed my library and a few personal items and moved to Anderson, Indiana. President Edwards had agreed that for the first year I could commute from Dayton, Ohio, since my oldest daughter was in her senior year of high school and would not graduate until May of 1996. I rented a small apartment in Anderson. My plan was to drive to Anderson each Monday morning and return home each Wednesday night. Then I would return to Anderson Thursday morning and go back to Dayton on Friday night for the weekend. Since I had resigned my position at the Salem Church of God, Debbie and I worshipped in Centerville, Ohio, at the new church we had recently planted. Julie and Amy continued at Salem Church of God with their friends who were part of the youth group.

Those early months in Anderson were lonely. I arrived in summer when most faculty, staff, and students were on summer break. To make matters worse, a few weeks after my arrival my secretary suffered a heart attack and was forced to take a six-month medical leave. Shortly after her return, she decided to retire and move out of state. Her absence forced me to look into file cabinets and locked closets to discover on my own what would have been readily accessible to my assistant.

From the beginning, it was apparent I was the new person in the building. My most supportive colleagues on the president's executive staff were on the other side of campus, which increased my sense of isolation. The seminary faculty and staff for the most part were older than I and had been around the School of Theology for many years. While they were always professional, I sensed some were disappointed that their new dean was not someone who had a track record in theological education. There is an old saying that faculty members "like to marry up." Faculty members, for the most part, prefer a Dean who is higher up the food chain of theological education and may be able to mentor them out of his years of experience.

But I was undaunted. While I had not spent my professional life in higher education, I had given the past twenty years to leading a large staff, raising budgets, and casting vision. That experience would prove useful here.

Early on, I recognized that the faculty was not only emotionally distant from me but from each other. Some had experienced traumatic disappointments in institutional life. To make matters worse, seminary enrollment was in a dramatic decline and faculty could see the handwriting on the wall. Would the seminary continue to exist? Was their long-term employment secure? Would the Church of God continue to invest financially in the seminary or cut it loose from budgetary support?

While I did not have a long pedigree of success in theological education, the faculty recognized that I did have a strong connection with President Edwards, the Board of Trustees, and many supporting congregations from which students and finances could flow. In my first year, I chose to focus on building relationships with the faculty, having informal lunches with them nearly every day of the week. Most faculty members did not eat lunch together but soon began to realize that something good was developing around table fellowship. I tried to discover what energized them, and then attempted to move them into assignments that aligned with their passions. I also advocated for increased personal and professional financial support. Financial support spoke volumes. These efforts improved morale and we began to function as a team!

In my second year, the trustees asked me to bring them a report regarding the School of Theology enrollment decline. I now attended trustee meetings where I spoke only when called upon, rather than sitting around the table asking others to report. It was evident the Board of Trustees now expected me to provide solutions to the institution's problems, not simply governance dialogue. The "honeymoon was over."

As the faculty's relational center began to improve, we blocked out time to address enrollment decline. We discovered that enrollment decline was an issue in most seminaries in North America from 1985 to 1995. Fewer and fewer young people were willing to consider Christian vocation but were going into more lucrative endeavors. After a thorough analysis we developed a plan to improve student life and student recruitment. The plan was presented to the trustees and resulted in a 137 percent increase in enrollment between 1998 and 2008.

However, seminaries in North America, including Anderson University School of Theology, witnessed another decline in enrollment beginning in 2009. Dan Aleshire, in 2014 the President of the Association of Theological Schools, wrote concerning the future of theological education, "There is almost no one who is unreservedly optimistic. I am more hopeful than worried and, every once in a while, unreservedly optimistic." It is my opinion theological schools that survive and thrive in the future will be those who are nimble enough to negotiate a changing landscape in both church and culture.

I was honored to serve for nineteen years as the Dean of Anderson University School of Theology, the longest tenure in the history of the school. If there was a word to best describe my years as dean, it would be *steward*. Anderson University School of Theology exists because people invested time, talent, and treasure in the ministry of graduate theological education. The Church of God has not always valued theologically prepared leaders, but we have benefited from women and men who have thought deeply about what we have received from God and are committed to pass on those treasures to future generations. My prayer is we never give up preparing women and men for the ministry of biblical reconciliation.

16. Ready or Not

In 1960, I began work in my father's service station at the age of twelve. I begged my dad to let me work so I could buy the Billy Martin baseball glove I had been eying in the local sporting goods store. He finally acquiesced and told me there were some floors to mop and toilets to clean. I got on my bicycle and rode to work, dreaming of my baseball glove. My dad soon discovered I really was helpful and allowed me to begin pumping gas. (I was too short to wash windshields.)

On Saturday, after six days of work, I was ready to retire. I planned to ride my bike to the sporting goods store to purchase my baseball glove. I'll never forget receiving ten crisp one-dollar bills for my six days of work. My dad also told me to report back to work on Monday. In his opinion, it was time for his youngest son to join my four older brothers and a brother-in-law in the family business.

Much to my surprise, my dad, who was also the church treasurer for 20 years, took one of the crisp dollar bills and told me I should put it the offering plate on Sunday morning. I still had nine dollars left and the baseball glove only cost seven, so I still had two dollars left. My dad explained how important tithing was and that lesson has stuck with me for a lifetime.

The next week, he took me by the bank where I opened a savings account. My dad told me to never spend all my money but to save some for a rainy day. (I still have my Barnitz Bank pass book.) Later in the summer he had me enroll in Social Security. My dad had lived through the Great Depression when older people had no financial resources when they could no longer physically work. My father was so pleased to know he would have Social Security to count on when he retired and he wanted me to be part of that American dream. I was not so enthused to contribute a portion of my pay each week to prepare for such a futuristic date of 2014. Now I am pleased that my dad, church treasurers, and Servant Solutions financial planners encouraged me to put money aside for the day I would stop working full time.

I know some people who say they intend to work until they breathe their last. Their work is their identity and the thought of not having a job is utterly alien. However, to work or not to work is not always our call to make. Some people must leave the workforce, ready or not, due to health

Anderson University School of Theology, Anderson, Indiana. I was the seventh dean of the School of Theology serving from 1995-2014.

concerns. Others face the stark reality of ending work, ready or not, because their business closes or their company moves to some distant part of the world and they are left behind. Still others are terminated, ready or not, because their skills are no longer needed. Ready or not, for one reason or another we all need to make plans for the future.

One of the greatest gifts we can leave our children or grandchildren will not be money in a bank account but the freedom of not having to provide financially for us in the future. No one knows what the future may bring. Sometimes we may need the financial help of family. However, trust in God, coupled with good financial planning, can help us to prepare for an uncertain financial future.

Debbie and I always prayed, "Lord, please help us to know when it is time to move on, and give us the grace to step out of the way and let others lead." As the old preacher of Ecclesiastes widely advised, "For everything there is a season." Early in the winter of 2014, I announced I would retire as dean effective July 1, 2014. It had been fifty-four years since my dad started me planning for retirement, and now the event sneaked up to announce, "Ready or not, I am here!"

17. The Bonus Years

Often during my work years, colleagues and I talked about what we would like to do in retirement, should we have health and strength to continue being productive. I had always imagined that I might return to congregational life and serve as a pastor or interim pastor. This next step seemed logical since I had served the church as pastor and theological educator for 39 years. Upon retirement, Anderson University gave me the title Dean Emeritus and Minister-at-Large and asked me to serve part-time with the university in the area of church relations. Over the years I had developed relationships with congregations, pastors, and Anderson University alumni, so this seemed an effective way for both Anderson University and me to continue serving our sponsoring church.

Also at the very top of my list was to be available to my children and grandchildren. I was never privileged to know my grandparents. Since I had been the youngest of seven siblings and Debbie and I began our family later in life, my daughters only knew my parents for a short period of time prior to their deaths. Our girls never knew Grandpa Jim, Debbie's father, who died an untimely death at the age of fifty-one.

Portrait unveiling on Tuesday, January 20, 2015. Pictured from left to right, President James Edwards, David Sebastian, Dean Emeritus and Minister-at-Large, and Artist David Slonim.

Julie and Amy were blessed to know their Grandma Dean, Debbie's mother, who lived to be ninety-six. Grandma Dean was a true gift to our girls. As long as the Lord gives us life and strength, we want to be available to our children and grandchildren.

Our grandchildren have never known Debbie and me as people who went to work like other people. Our relationships with our grandchildren will be based upon who we are, not what we do. While this seems a bit odd after a lifetime of work, this is a role we readily embrace!

Our first and oldest granddaughter, Mary Katherine Sebastian Short, daughter of Colin and Julie, was born in Phoenix, Arizona, on June 8, 2009. While her grandparents, aunts, and uncles on both sides of the family lived in the Midwest, they traveled to Arizona for her birth. When Mary Kate arrived in this world, after a difficult labor, she was surrounded by a loving family who welcomed our very first grandchild. How proud we all were! Mary Kate is an outgoing child, always trying new things and keeping us entertained through her various endeavors.

Julie and Colin's second child, Matthew Wesley Sebastian Short, captured our hearts from day one. At the time of Matthew's birth, Debbie, Julie and I were all working at Anderson University. Julie had a pregnancy crisis at work, so Debbie and I were called to drive her to St. Johns Hospital, where Colin would meet us as he raced home from work in Indianapolis. Julie was then transferred to St Vincent Women's Hospital in Indianapolis, where she was assigned bed rest for the next month. Our daily prayers now included Julie, Colin, Mary Kate, and their unborn baby boy.

On June 7, 2012, our family's first baby boy arrived. His time in ICCU was longer than expected. It was difficult to watch him attached to so many monitors and machines. Matthew was much slower than his big sister to begin speaking, but since he started talking he has not stopped! Our lives have been blessed by our super-hero grandson.

Jon and Amy returned from living in California in October of 2009. One day Jon and Amy stopped by the house to visit. To my surprise, Amy gave me a "For Sale" sign and asked if I would be willing to help Jon sell his Harley Davidson motorcycle while he was gone on tour. I was caught off guard because I knew Jon loved his motorcycle, but when Amy handed me the "For Sale" sign I saw a mischievous look in her eye. The sign was Jon and Amy's way of telling us she was pregnant and would be giving birth to their first child in December. Luca Dean McLaughlin was born December 9, 2012, in Indianapolis. Amy also had a difficult labor, but Luca soon brought inexpressible joy to our family. Luca has a great imagination. She loves to dress up like a princess and enjoys telling and hearing scary bedtime stories.

We were saddened but not surprised to hear that Jon and Amy would be moving to Nashville, Tennessee. Jon is a musician, so Nashville was a logical location for his work. It was in Nashville that Jon and Amy would have their second child, Liv

Harlow McLaughlin, who was born on July 29, 2015. From my perspective, it was a very rough and scary birth for Liv and delivery for Amy. While mothers have been giving birth to children for a long time, this grandpa was traumatized by the birth of each grandchild!

The Indiana family members on both sides were present in Nashville for the birth of Liv. As years passed, we learned that Liv is a risk taker who has no fear. She believes she can and should do everything her big sister does. When we travel to Nashville for a visit, Liv is always ready to show us one of her new daredevil tricks; but I'm happy to say she likes to cuddle with her grandpa just like her mother did as a toddler.

We always heard that being a grandparent is even better than being a parent. Let me add my voice to the chorus: It is great to be a grandparent!

Another bonus for retirement has been the opportunity to do some travel. Debbie and I had determined we wanted to get out of the cold of winter for a period of time to enjoy sunshine and warm temperatures someplace south. We had lived in Florida and Arizona and have friends in both plac-

Grandchildren celebrating birthday 69 with grandpa. Grandchildren from left to right are Mary Kate Short, Luca Dean McLaughlin, Liv Harlow McLaughlin and Matthew Wesley Short.

es, so those locations were always on our radar screen for places to winter. However, we also want to visit Texas, southern California, Costa Rica, Grand Cayman, and Mexico in search of warm climates.

One travel experience we want to share is a family trip to the Holy Land. Debbie and I visited the Holy Land earlier in life and found it to be a spiritually rich experience to walk where Jesus walked. We want to take such a pilgrimage with our children and grandchildren, hoping it will provide a lifetime of memories that strengthen their Christian faith. We want the grandchildren to be old enough to remember the trip while at the same time we are young enough to remember it!

Debbie and I have decided to engage our brains in retirement by learning the Spanish language. Each day begins by doing a Spanish lesson at home. Our dream is to do a Spanish language immersion experience in Costa Rica at a school that trains missionaries. While we have no official call to world mission, we believe that learning the Spanish language will help in our mission to be good neighbors.

18. A Credo of Hope

Herb, one of my older brothers, was a builder and racer of hotrods and dragsters. When I was about seven years old, I watched him work on one of his hotrods and asked, "What is the first thing you do when building a car you are going to race?" Without pause, he said, "The first thing I do is work on the brakes. It doesn't matter how fast you go, if you can't stop, you are in big trouble!"

Whether he said that to me tongue-in-cheek I do not know. I took him quite literally because it made perfect sense to me. Others have said, "Always work with the end in mind." In other words, where is this course of action ultimately taking me? Consequences are real, so we need to plan accordingly.

This morning as I write, it is Christmas, a day when millions of people around the world celebrate the birth of Jesus. We sing and celebrate the good news that God's Word became flesh and visited our planet. Jesus, God in the flesh came to show us how to live so that someday we may live with him in heaven forever.

People have responded to the Jesus story in different ways. Some have said Jesus never existed. They believed his story

Big brother Herb Sebastian, cofounder of the Pacemaker Auto Club, Middletown, Ohio. When as a boy I asked what was the first thing he did when building a race car? He said, "Install good brakes!"

was manufactured by simple minds a kind of wish fulfillment. Today, very few people believe the Jesus story is a manufactured tale. Today some argue that Jesus was real but He was not God in the flesh. Jesus for some was simply a Jewish peasant who went about helping people to comprehend a new way of living and relating. Jesus, in the view of some people was one of many religious leaders trying to make this world a better place.

I believe that Jesus is the second person of the Christian Trinity. Jesus was fully God and fully man. He came to earth and lived a perfect life, not simply as an example to follow but as the Son of God, the perfect and only sacrifice for our sinful lives. Therefore, since Jesus is God and has invited me to believe in him as the way, the truth, and the life, I put my trust in him for this life and the life that is to come.

When I was eleven years old, at the conclusion of a Wednesday evening prayer meeting on August 5, 1959, I began my journey with Jesus. That night I gave as much of myself that I knew to as much of Jesus as I could comprehend. When I was in the eighth grade at the age of thirteen, I was baptized. During my adolescent years my devotion to the way of Jesus waned. While I always believed in Jesus, sometimes my behavior was not what it should have been. In high school and later in the Army, I was what some might call "a secret Christian." My light of witness was at best hidden under a bushel. While not succumbing to peer pressure to get involved in a lot of dangerous activities, I was not living a bold Christian life.

After marriage, Debbie and I, along with some friends, attended a lay witness training event at the Salem Church of God in Dayton, Ohio. There I experienced the infilling of the Holy Spirit by faith. I had at an early age accepted the gift of eternal life when I put my trust in Jesus. Now I was being invited to give myself fully to the sanctifying work of the Holy Spirit. This moment of surrender was the first of many times of consecration in my adult years. The ministry of the Holy Spirit has been a source of guidance in life decisions. The Holy Spirit has also been a source of conviction when I failed to live up to what I know. Through confession and consecration, I am seeking to walk in the Spirit.

Another moment of divine awareness came when I was a young adult and was asked to teach an adult bible class. The study would center in the Gospel of Matthew. I had taught young children and youth but I was a little nervous about teaching adults. I went to my pastor and asked for guidance about teaching adults. At the end of our conversation, he gave me a Bible commentary and told me to first study the text for myself but then in my preparation I should consult a Bible commentary to compare my thoughts with other people who have thought long and hard about the biblical text. To this point in my life, I had not seen or read a Bible commentary, so I was fascinated to read the social and historical background of the biblical text. I was introduced to contemporaries of Jesus. I encountered first-

and second-century writers outside of the Bible who referenced Jesus of Nazareth as a historical figure who lived in Palestine and gained a following of disciples.

My study of the book of Matthew became a turning point in my life as the commentary by William Barclay opened my eyes of faith in a new way. I began to realize the Bible and subsequently my faith were grounded in history, not simply imagination. To that point, my faith in Jesus had been something like my former belief in Santa Claus. In my mind, Jesus and Santa Claus were good and wholesome semi-historical figures with a tradition that was nice to hand down to others, but with no significance for my daily life. My faith had been consumed as milk but now a much more satisfying meat was before me. In many ways, I learned more in my role as an adult Sunday school teacher than any of the adult participants in my class.

In college, this love for teaching led me to do a double major in Bible and Christian Education. I discovered the Bible, particularly the New Testament, pointed to an existence beyond this life. From the beginning, belief in a life beyond has always been part of human societies. But within societies ancient and modern, there have also been stark voices reminding us there is no concrete proof of life beyond what we now experience, so we might as well "eat, drink and be merry for tomorrow we die."

I believe the Christian faith teaches that there is an existence beyond death. I also believe, to borrow a phrase from Tom Wright, that "there is life after life after death." Over the years I have read many books about near-death experiences. I have heard about people who have gone to heaven and returned. I have listened to folks talking about communicating with deceased loved ones. I've seen movies about dying people being drawn to a bright light. I do not base my hope on these personal encounters. I try to square my belief about the life to come with what I understand scripture to teach.

I believe that when a true Christian dies the believer is consciously present with the Lord in paradise. I do not believe *paradise* is a synonym for heaven. Jesus said to the thief on the cross, "Today you shall be with me in paradise" (Luke 23:43). The apostle Paul also reminds us that we are either "at home in the body" or "at home with the Lord" (2 Cor. 5:6, 8). Whatever and wherever this paradise is, we know it is a good place because we are with the Lord. However, the Bible also speaks about another existence after death often described as a great separation from God. Hell is sometimes described in the Bible as a kind of existence on earth, like the smoldering fires of Gehenna, a dump outside of ancient Jerusalem, which was a place of utter despair. But hell is also described as a place of punishment for those who choose not to embrace and live out the good news of the gospel (see 2 Pet. 2:4-10).

    I believe at the end of the age, on the Day of Judgment, all people will give an account of their lives. There will be a singular resurrection of the body of believers and non-believers. The book of Matthew uses the metaphor of the separation of the sheep and the goats (Matt. 25:32-33). The sheep are assigned to life everlasting with God. The goats are assigned to life everlasting without God. The believer's newly resurrected body will not be a resuscitation of the old earthly body but a new body like the resurrected body of Jesus. John writes, "It does not yet appear what we shall be: but we know that, when he shall appear, we shall be like him; for we shall see him as he is" (1 John 3:2).

The newly resurrected body of the non-believer will be assigned to hell. Hell is always described in negative and destructive terms. In Luke's parable of Lazarus and Dives (Luke 16:19-31), hell (Hades) is even described as a place of torment (v. 23). The parable connects the actions in this life with the life that is to come. Hell is a place to be avoided.

As a pastor and theological educator, I have read and discussed many different theories about heaven and hell. I know some people have difficulty believing that either place exists. Some like to think heaven is a place where all people go when they die. Some dislike the idea that anyone, even someone evil such as Adolph Hitler or Osama Bin Laden, will go to hell if it is a place of eternal punishment. But the Bible and the ancient Christian creeds speak plainly of heaven and hell, whether those concepts fit with modern sensibilities or not. Some have simply chosen to agree to disagree about such ultimate matters. The Bible encourages us to not neglect our salvation and advises that, from beginning to end, we work out our salvation with fear and trembling (Phil. 2:12).

Rodney Stark, distinguished Professor of Social Sciences at Baylor University, writes in his book, *Why God (?)*: "Anyone with good sense would believe in God because that is a no-loss proposition. God either exists or does not exist, and people have the choice of either believing in God or not. This results in four combinations. Assuming that God exists, then upon death those who believe will gain all the rewards promised to the faithful and escape the costs imposed on the unfaithful. In contrast, the unbelievers will miss out on the rewards and receive the punishments. Now, assume there is no God. When they die, believers will simply be dead. But so will those who didn't believe." Building on the work of philosopher Blaise Pascal in *Pensees*, Stark reasoned, "The smart move is to believe, for one has everything to gain, but nothing to lose."

While this is surely not the only argument for believing in and serving God, it is one of many arguments that encourage us to live with the end in mind. As a minister of the gospel, with the end in mind, I choose to believe and proclaim that there is a heaven to gain and a hell to avoid. As with Paul, "I am not ashamed of the gospel, because it is the power of God that brings salvation to everyone that believes: first to the Jew, then to the Gentile" (Rom. 1:16).

Epilogue

In my early elementary-school years, I wanted to be a cowboy. I dreamed of living on a ranch, riding horses, and shooting guns at bad guys. My heroes were Roy Rogers, the Lone Ranger, Fury, Spin and Marty. I desired Western wear and lassoes and wanted nothing to do with Sunday suits and lassies. Strangely, I had never been out West and didn't know a single cowboy. My cowboy vision was solely the work of a new enterprise called television sponsored by Cheerios, Wonder Bread and Ovaltine.

Radio and television shaped the lives of most baby boomers. We looked to trusted figures to tell us the news, remind us what was in fashion, and inform our opinions. Most of us, if we heard of computers, only thought of them as huge devices hidden away in large rooms processing information for giant conglomerates. We never thought of them as life companions speaking into our lives everywhere we would go. In the 1960s and 1970s, we discovered facts by going to the library and accessing information through the Dewey decimal system. What pastors and theological educators longed for were books, commentaries, encyclopedias, and journals so that they could be wise sages in the sanctuary or lecture hall. The information age has changed this paradigm forever.

In over forty years of ministry, in both church and academy, I have had the opportunity to see many changes in Christian ministry. Two things I have noticed about change: Change is inevitable and change is often perceived as loss. In 1975, my ordination service into Christian ministry was held at the Glendale Church of God located on 62nd Avenue in Indianapolis, Indiana, where I served as associate pastor. During retirement, in 2017, I was invited to return to this same congregation as interim pastor. The congregation was now located at Keystone at the Crossing (on Haverstick) and was known as "The Church at the Crossing." Most of the congregation in 2017 did not know or remember the turmoil of the relocation or the angst of the name change. Now the location and the church name are the norms, so life and ministry move forward.

This return to the place where I began my ministry was a wonderful opportunity to reflect, not simply about the changes that had taken place in one congregation, but about the many changes that have taken place in the life of the Church of God in the United States over the past forty plus years. During those forty years I have had opportunity to serve fourteen congregations, either as a full-time or interim pastor.

One change has been the turning away from a national movemental loyalty and a return to autonomous congregational loyalty. In the Church of God at the dawn of the twentieth century, there was widespread bias against national and international ministries. However, in the 1950s, 1960s, and 1970s, there was a tendency to believe that we could accomplish more for Christ if we pooled our resources and allowed national leaders to coordinate the mission of local assemblies. In the post-Christian, post-denominational era of the past thirty years, Church of God congregations once again became convinced that mission decisions should be made closer to home.

However, as I write this memoir, there seems to be a renewed desire by some to return to a more centralized organization of mission and ministry. Will there be another shift in the locus of authority? Only time will tell.

Another personal observation is that worship services have changed in style and structure. In my beginning years of ministry, sanctuaries with oak pulpits, stained-glass windows, organs, pianos, and choirs with robes were the standard fare. Today, church architecture can be more likened to commercial retail space with a few overt Christian symbols. In my early pastoral ministry, the theology of the congregation was shaped by strong biblical/doctrinal exposition. Hymns and anthems helped teach the church about the nature of the triune God. The charismatic movement of the 1960s and 1970s brought a new emphasis in worship, encouraging people to experience God rather than simply to know the attributes of God. Worship teams of that generation utilized contemporary musical instruments such as guitars, drums, and electronic keyboards along with mood-setting lights and high-decibel audio. Most of these innovations are still with us.

Many current church-goers believe that preaching is too authoritative. They prefer a more democratized, conversational team teaching approach to communicate the gospel.

The corporate emphasis on customer service has also subtly impacted the church. Forty years ago, to borrow a phrase from President Kennedy, Christians were encouraged to "ask not what the church can do for you but what you can you do for the church." In later years, we have encouraged the laity to rediscover the reformation principle of the priesthood of believers. As a result, congregants now want to see a return on their investment of time and resources, and lay leaders have resolved "to discover and meet the needs of people." For better or worse, they no longer look to a single congregational leader for ministry vision but to a host of teachers, bloggers, and opinionated friends. Customer service has also changed the way congregational members choose to give financially. Today, congregants are less inclined to give to the congregation's general budget but to specific causes that strike a personal chord.

I have also noticed that congregations place a greater emphasis on social concerns; however, they often apply social litmus tests to determine the validity of a local congregation. While in the past churches had doctrinal and social positions on important issues, these positions were summarized in written documents for reflection, discussion, and action. Our current social-media environment emphasizes political and cultural wars, often forcing church members to take extreme positions rather than coming to the center. Isaiah the prophet encouraged the people of God, "Come now, let us reason together, says the Lord; though your sins are like scarlet, they shall be white as snow; though they are red like crimson, they shall become like wool" (Isa. 1:18). Coming to the center requires us to be informed not only about our personal doctrinal and social positions but also about the positions of others. Rock-solid arguments seldom change minds, but "speaking the truth in love we are to grow up in all aspects into him who is the head even Christ" (Eph. 4:15). We need to remember that "knowledge puffs up but love builds up" (1 Cor. 8:1).

In my lifetime, the church has experienced the blessing of change. It has also suffered because of change. When I had opportunity to return to the congregation where I began my ministry, I observed that the people were still experiencing significant change, yet they were still committed to Christ and the church. I saw multi-generational families still worshipping God, still teaching the young, still serving at home and abroad, and still loving each other. I saw people who have weathered change but who have not given up on their faith in Jesus and their love for each other.

God led me from being a mechanic to being a minister. I recognize that being a minister is not and should not be everybody's vocation. Regardless of our occupation, we are called to deny self, take up the cross daily, and follow Jesus. Our task in daily life—whether at home, work, school, church, or the community at large—is to live out the gospel story in word and deed. Moreover, as occasions allow, we invite other people to embrace the gospel story.

Denying self, taking up our cross daily, and following Jesus is a difficult calling that often goes against the grain of modern American culture. Sometimes we feel alone and are tempted to give up, walk away, or embrace a watered-down version of the gospel. When you find yourself in that predicament, I encourage you never to give up. You have too much to gain and too much to lose if you turn away from Jesus' story of redemption to embrace another story. One song I have requested to be sung at my funeral contains the following words:

*I love to tell the story of unseen things above
of Jesus and His glory, of Jesus and His love.
I love to tell the story, because I know 'tis true;
it satisfies my longings as nothing else can do.**

Nothing in life would bring me more satisfaction than for my wife, children, grandchildren, extended family, acquaintances, and the whole world to embrace the gospel story and never give up!

---

*Katherine Hankey, "I Love to Tell the Story," *Worship the Lord: Hymnal of the Church of God* (Anderson, IN: Warner Press, 1989), 361.